*Terminalia*

## ALSO BY DANIEL MENAKER:

*Friends and Relations: A Collection of Stories*

*The Worst* (with Charles McGrath)

*The Old Left and Other Stories*

*The Treatment*

*A Good Talk: The Story and Skill of Conversation*

*My Mistake: A Memoir*

*The African Svelte: Ingenious Misspellings that Make Surprising Sense*

# TERMINALIA

*poems*

DANIEL MENAKER

Published 2020 by Portal Press

Distributed by n+1 Foundation

P.O. Box 26428, Cadman Plaza Station

Brooklyn, NY 11202-9021

www.nplusonemag.com/terminalia

ISBN 978-1-953813-00-8

Printed by the Sheridan Press

Manufactured in the United States of America

Design by Rachel Ossip

First Printing

FOR LAURA SILLERMAN

# CONTENTS

## PART VI: RESUMPTION

## PART V: TERMINALIA

# PART I

# OVERTURE

# DIAGNOSIS

## 1.

"Anything else," says Dr. B. "I don't
think so," you reply. "Oh, well, right here
there is some sensitivity." You tap
your upper abdomen, and then the doctor
does. A lot. "Have you eaten in
the last few hours?" "No," you say, "I forgot."
He says, "There's an imaging place nearby—
I'll call and see if they can take a picture.
Just in case."

You go. They put you on the slab—as in
a morgue is what you think—and flee to
their glass-fronted, ray-proof bunker.
They slide you into the hole, the way they do
a body for cremation, but quickly
slide you out again. You hear the bunker
door reopen and the nurse is by
your side, annoyed. It's not my fault, you
want to say but don't. "The image isn't
clear enough," she says. "We need some iodine."
She injects it and you feel hot
and need to piss. Back in the hole
again and now you're done.
On your way out, the person at the desk
says, "Dr. B. would like to see you at

his office right away." Do you say
Uh-oh? No—you decide good news
must be what he will give to you.

Wrong!, as your friend Topper always says.
"Good news or bad?" you ask him as
you walk the hall that leads to his office.
His arm is tight around your shoulder.
"Bad," he says, taking his arm away,
walking ahead of you. Après-farewell and the clearest
sign of love, is what you think, as you
begin your long negotiation with the truth.


## 2.


A one-lane low-way,
a sheet-white truck coming at you,
from about a mile away.
On both sides drop-offs.
And anyway, the wheel won't turn.
The brakes? Tapioca.
The key? Soldered.
The doors? None.
The windows? $8\frac{1}{2} \times 11$.
Press here to submit.

# PART II

# REIFICATION

## SHARPS

Here's the question: You can't
share needles, but can you reuse
them yourself—the little guys—
for insulin? With your pancreass
o'ermastered by its own perversity,
your blood will be a glucose syrup,
completing your acquisition
of the farm before you're
set to leave this nice apartment.

So one shot in the morning of this,
one before meals of that. Four, all told.
Laborious. Peel back the paper,
take off the bigger cap.
Take off the small one—tiny, rigid,
condomesque in shape.
Inject in thigh or abdomen,
Sat., right, Sun., left, et cetera.
The chances of infection
from reuse low to zero.
How much easier to put back
the little plastic sleeve than
to begin anew each time.

Not much. Just a way
to try to try to game
a system you can't game.

No one can, in the long run.
(In your case, the short.)

(You've had the cheating in you almost
from the start. Latin III, Mr.
Callahan caught you out with
"Acta deos numquam mortalia fallunt,"
and other tiny prompts written on
a tiny piece of paper palmed—poorly,
it turned out—in your left [*sinistra*] hand.
How perfect, it turned out! "Mortal
actions never fool the gods.")

## NAPSTER

Give in, give in!
Get some practice for forever,
even though it has no dreams,
good or bad.

Or so it seems.

## BIOPSY

Emmylou, in the air, softly
but just loud enough:
"Tougher Than the Rest."
"That's me," you say silently
out loud. It's the Fentanyl.
Then her and The Band:
"Evangeline." "How did they *know*?"
you say out loud silently.
This Fentanyl, if only for the nonce,
("nonce"? really?), makes the cancer
worth it, while the doctor is
doing something to your abdomen.
"Nemodba," you say to flesruoy.

Likewise briefly, these small mercies—
The floaty high,
The gawjus nurses,
The doorman's long, sincere embrace
when you get home and clue him in—
redeem the ordeal. But
"Briefly," you say again, out loud.
And so does doing this
for you and others, or
so you hope.
Or is it "fool yourself"?
You, we, are always looking
for Alleviation in this life—

I've learned you get what you can get.
The Analgesic Permanente.
Even when we know
it comes only at the end.

# BLOOD WORK

"Robert! Robert Menaker," the technician calls out.
(Maybe later, if anyone cares,
I'll explain about the name.)

The people in the waiting room
have every aspect:

1. Reading the paper
with an intensity
born of their own urgencies,
you suspect (you detached observer, you).

2. Wearing facemasks, as if
in a horror movie,
which is in some ways what this is,
except for the "movie" part.

3. 45°, mouth agape. "Ah-gah-pay,"
your mother told you once, means
"the highest form of love."
Or maybe it was twice.
"I will disown you if you ever say
'Tiffany's' again," she also told you.
"It's 'Tiffany.'"

4. Talking with animation,
often to friends newfound

within these trenches,
the company that proximity
+ misery + danger frequently demand.
Their only riflery is patience.

5. 180°. Escape.
Or bad shape.

"Robert!"
"Coming," you call,
And you go in and sit down
behind a curtain, for
The veins inspected,
The needle,
The compliment to the nurse
For a painless puncture (which
actually hurt a lot, you phony).

You watch the tubes—three?
Really!? Wait—*four?*—
fill, with what's left of your life's blood,
which was given to you by your mother
and your father. And here is another
small even if automatic mercy:

They are not here to see this, detached observers now,
as they were to see your brother's death
at twenty-nine. No full recovery
from that but some salvage washed ashore.

## ROBERT *(by Robert Daniel Menaker)*

We—my brother, Mike, and I—
called our parents "Mame" and
"Bobby," parental first-name-ism
being the forties' lefty vogue.
So why they named me Robert
baffles me to this late day.
In any case, to avoid this Self-
Inflicted Bob confusion, I was Danny.
But in leases, licenses, and probably
my own upcoming certificate of
expiration, so as to be legally dead,
I am and will be Robert. As I am,
on every second Wednesday, for the needle
and its temporarily time-buying poison.

("Danny Boy," the grownups at your uncle's camp
would say to and even warble at you,
so often as to drive you nuts. But
now the pipes indeed are calling—
and pretty loudly, at that—and the
song becomes anthemic and funereal and
grand. And if you are not alone,
you must turn away and hide your eyes.)

## WAITING-AND-WAITING-AND-WAITING-ROOM PATIENT PANCREAS LAB REPORT

In the upper left quadrant,
behind the recyclables,
two mice shooting craps.
Behind them, a food cart—halal.
On the right, three (my resident says four)
fleas dancing to a roundelay—a hybrid of
Scottish drurgh and Malaysian tondo.
"What on earth is *that*?" says my resident.

The lower-left quadrant, deteriorated to angel-food cake.
(My resident cries out, "Improved!")
Lower-right gone missing, found later—by a nurse's aide—
under the bed, at play with the remote,

maybe trying to find a live organ recital.

## FURLOUGH

"We can skip this time,"
 says Dr. Varghese.
"And reduce the dosage
 when you come back.
 The bloodwork is good."

All the way to their
East over here, from
the Hudson and your West,
only to be released this time around?
Will you take it or what?
Your wife, your center of gravity
and the geometer of these crosstown/
downtown voyages,
grins and murmurs, "If you insist."

Back out on Third Avenue
from the sepulchral quiet
of the poison palace's
cabbage walls and doody-and-gray
décor, here is a food truck, panels
plastered with vibrant shots
of lamb over rice, fish over rice—
like a children's poem.
"Both are nice," you say to yourself.
"And will suffice."

"Halal!" you call out, and
the upper-half-only dark man
rushing this way and that—
the line is long, the time is lunch—
laughs and calls "Halal!"

Third and Lex and 53rd
loom up before you,
overwhelming in their
signage, vehicles, and clamor,
to say nothing of the traffic in the air—
though you just did say something of it,
didn't you, you tell yourself and chuckle.
All for you alone, it feels like
a panorama of release. "Two whole weeks
without the needles," your wife says now.
"Seems like forever."
"Nay, madam,"
you reply. "I know not 'seems.'"

## SHARPS II

Here's the question: You can't
share needles but can you reuse
them for yourself—the little guys—
for insulin? With your pancreass
o'ermastered by its own perversity,
your blood will be a glucose syrup
completing acquisition of the farm
before you're set to leave this nice
apartment, if you ever are.

So one shot in the morning of this,
one before meals of that. Four, all told.
Laborious. Peel back the paper,
unscrew the bigger plastic cap.
Remove the smaller one—tiny, rigid,
condomesque in shape.
Inject in thigh or abdomen:
Sat., right, Sun., left, et cetera.
The chances of infection
from reuse low to zero.
How much easier to replace
the little plastic sleeve than
begin again each time.

Not much. Just a way
to cheat, to try to game
a system you can't game.

No one can, in the long run,
or in your case, the short.

We're never off the hook.
We get away with nothing.

# PART III

# RECESS

## ADJUVANTS

They pay respects before they're owed, your
friends who, these two no-infusion
weeks, come to see you, in your baseball
hat and new, 32 jeans, down from 34,
and, before that, 35. Maybe even 36,
when you yourself were 36.

Some are nervous and sit straight,
like recent converts to a cause.
One looks relaxed, his wife "relaxed."
And one is genuinely jolly—"You can't
check out," he says, "until you've been excused."

Right away or later on, most want
to know the clinicals.
(But "How long?" with trepidation,
if at all.) You fill them in.
"Bilirubin." "MRI." "Diffuse."
"Referred clavicular discomfort."
"Nocturia," you conclude, to the
jolly fellow. "A Mozart étude"
is what he says—"if I am not mistaken."

These are relaxants for your guests,
these recitations of the argot
of the docs and lab reports.
Like the liturgy in church,

like any chant, like any pause
in turbulence aloft,
or a mile or so of smoother road.

They also work on you, the facts.
They are hard and real,
and, in company with—
Oh, all right!—a Mozart étude—
make manifest the best of what we do.

Calm always settles
on the conversation then—
a kind of silent truce between
the facts and death,
with caritas the referee.

It's only later, when they're gone,
you begin once more to weep
with joy and its twin brother, mourning.
This can't go on forever.

## GRACE

You are thankful for your
children—period.
And for the women with
the courage to
allow their being here.

Your son—thirty-what, again?
Handsome, bearded like them all
these days. He's sure he's Irish
in descent and loves it that they
threw the British out.

(You went to Dublin twenty years ago,
you and he, and visited Kilmainham Gaol,
where he was struck stone-silent, reverential,
by the wall in front of which
almost twenty rebels fell to fame.)
Later on, the publican: "Are you
eighteen?" And Will replied, "Today!"
"A pint for you, then, on the house,
and maybe even for your dad.
I have to think about it. He *is*
your dad, right? Are we sure?"

And grateful for your daughter, Lizi—
*her* spelling, you remind yourself.
She is also thirty-um-three? four?

(In her practice, Lizi works with clients
who are disturbed, this way or that:
Voices, shyness, family oppression.
More than one with scars upon their wrists.)
The Glarer glared at her for many sessions
and every time that Lizi asked her something
would reply, "I don't know—that's *your* job."
But Lizi kept her cool, finally reduced the Glare.

And thankful for your wife, Katherine,
with her good sense and looks
and company and concern
for you and those she leads—
the deaf. They would be even more invisible
if not for her. (She advocates when she's
asleep, I swear. She cannot hear herself,
I think, but I can.)

And for everything you are *not* grateful for:
turndowns, social slights, your cowardice,
anxieties, the three ectopic pregnancies
that served to bring your kids to you.
Even your brother's awful death, at twenty-nine,
which began to make a man of you at last.
And even for your parlous situation,
at least from time to time.
For it has brought you back to this.

## ACCOMPANIMENT

We can't put music into poetry,
and when poetry is set to music,
it becomes a jingle.
You're thinking this, on this
last day before resumption
of the poison medicine, because you want to
listen to your favorite, "Three Chords
and the Truth" on the Sonos—given
to you by your son last Christmas,
when you had your hair and cared
about store closings up on Broadway.

So, what to listen to this last day
before the food starts once again to
taste like from a midden in Peru,
and your bowels seize, your throat
swells up, your shoulder aches
because your liver
presses up against the nerves that
lead there—some nerve!—and
your mouth is blossoming with sores?

Irish! "The Rising of the Moon."
Defiance, triumph over
overwhelming odds. "Bold Riley," too:
"Goodbye, my darlin', goodbye, my dear-o,
Bold Riley-o has gone away."

And "Your Long Journey,"
(*q*.G),* O'Carolan, Lead Belly,
Blind Reverend Gary Davis, whom
you introduced at Folk Festival long ago
and who said, when a girl walked by,
"You lookin' *mighty* good today, child.")

You are now in tears again.
Like poetry, music can hold things
together when you are falling apart,
in this case at the beginning of literally:
the bunches of hair on the pillow.
You get up. "Like snow," your wife says,
as you and she make the bed in the morning.
"But not," you say. "More like hair."
And she laughs.

This weeping differs from the other,
for, like poetry, music serves to answer
death and our condition's chaos:
It lasts, assembles things, and says,
"People may forget, but what you're
hearing now, and maybe even writing,
will not be forgotten. Go ahead and cry."

*(*q*.G): "Which Google"—your own coinage,
or so you've let yourself believe.

## THAT SAME NIGHT

You have a dream—quite the dream!
But before you try to put it here, you must
admit distrust of dream recitals. Poetry
is bad enough, all on its own—
"I will arise and go now." ("And
none too soon," you mutter.)
Poetry about a dream (except perhaps
for "Kubla Khan," by that trinominal
opiater Coleridge, if it's really based
on a druggy dream, as many have surmised)
is cream on ice cream. Ketchup on
tomatoes. Small waves on smaller water.

Nevertheless, the dream:

The city—some city—is as if
interrupted. Cops doze in their cars,
planes take off but never land.
Traffic lights blink yellow all the time.
The diner's out of coffee. Conversation
on the street is
"What can I tell you?"
"It's like everything else."
"You know it, pal."
"Like I was saying."
Office workers struggle with their
documents. The print's too small,

the figures won't add up.
Moms and dads at home are at a loss—
schools are closed.

You take a walk. The theater just up
the block is shuttered, but an old guy
in a carny barker outfit standing there
points at you and beckons you in,
and you go in. You are alone. The seat
is luxury, the "Armrests Fully Self-
Adjusting," says the first thing on the
ginormous screen, and they are.

Then it says, "The Show!" in letters a thousand
times the size of these, letters shifting in what you didn't
even know are your favorite fonts,
didn't even know they were your favorites,
didn't know you knew their names,
because you didn't, in your waking life.
First this one, of course—Times New Roman—
and then a hundred others, each in its actual
caparison:

> **THE SHOW** (Algerian)
> **The Show** (Bodoni MT Black)
> *The Show* (Harlow Solid Italic)
> *The Show* (Kunstler Script)
> The Show (Chiller)
> Etc. (er, Times New Roman)

They stand for Choice, is what you realize.
So you decide to stick with TNR
(AND LAMENT THAT ALGERIAN
APPEARS TO HAVE NO LOWER CASE,
and that Goudy Old Style—a great name—
looks, boringly, very much like this).

The screen—a 3D portal to the vast
alternative—now shows your life.
Your lives, because you see
not only everything that has been but all
that would have been, had you
married Chloe, learned the mandolin,
moved to San Francisco when the chance arose.
Fallen off the back of the truck you almost
fell off when you were twelve, been crippled by
the polio you never knew, till now, you had.
Had different kids, better health, worse health,
left your wife, been left, turned left, turned right,
turned on, kept straight.

There were a few vast
differences—dying young, being fired, getting
very lucky in the market.
Outliers, all of them, though all looked
logical. Everything did, because, well,
A life's a life, you understood now. You get
what you gave to get. The illness you're fighting
and to which you will lose was Written, like this.

Uneditable, inevitable, as fated as, for now, your

Waking.

# PART IV

# RESUMPTION

# JETSAM

As Nurse Luddy turns the little dials and
opens the tubes and presses the buttons and
turns the beeper on, and checks the screens
and calls a colleague in to verify and repeat
instructions and checks your name and date
of birth ("Tell me your name and date of birth,"
she says, and you, you clown, you say
"Your name and date of birth")—
As all that is going forward, you marvel
at the amount of stuff that's being thrown
away as the processes proceed:
gowns, masks, plastic bags, plastic tubes,
cellophanic caps, cardboard packaging,
nitrile gloves.

No more items in a series here, at least for now—
A sad and easy excuse for poetry.
Well, OK, except for this:

## REFLECTIONS ABOUT THE LIST ABOVE
1. The awful mess made to save your life,
   and for so short a time.
2. Oh! Did you get up and leave? Nobody saw you.
3. Whoso list to hunt, I know where is an hind.
4. Lists, as in this poem, are efforts to contain
   the uncontainable, like picture frames (are there
      no walls?) and final scenes in plays and movies.

(the unkilled characters have lives to live) and
underpants and these garbage cans that the nurses,
are filling up, "shave-and-a-haircut," when Lester
Holt says good night, a child's arms outspread
 beneath the cosmos, wedding ceremonies,
workouts, warfare, wishful thinking,
initial-letter repetitions, obituaries,
birth announcements, Brian Greene's
description of the atomization of
the universe in three trillion years,
more or less. Because—really?
Nothing will happen after that?
Will time be discontinued then?
Did it really ever begin, Big Bang
notwithstanding?

You have to keep a hotpack on your arm
when they switch from the relatively
tolerable stuff to gemcitabine, which
will begin to sting if the site's unwarmed.
You take the hotpack (more plastic, natch)
and smack it somewhere and it heats up
somehow and after twenty minutes cools off.
And then you smack the second, wear it like
some ermine of the arm, and throw the first away.

## BIOPSY REDUX

Fentanyl again, and the white, warm loaf of
soft cloths on your tummy, peen, and ballusteros.
"To keep you warm," the nurse says. "What else?"
you say. She doesn't take offense
but laughs and says, "If you want cold . . ."
The pathologist, a different one who
has commandeered the other's beard
and youth and somber mien,
swabs around down there and starts
the excavation. This time it's Bach
quietly afloat above, a Brandenburg.
"A Brandy Berg," you say aloud, drunk,
the one that starts, Da-da-dot, da-da-dot,
Da-da-dot, da-da-dot, da-da-dot, dot
Da-da-da-da-da-da-da-da-dot.
Oh, come on, you know it, or would
if you were here, and if you know
those concertos, concertis, concertorinos
and were drugged up like this
but not so disconcerted. Heh-heh.
The nurse smiles and asks, "What's funny?"

Bach above, your nice warm balls below.
The time before, when Beard One was done,
he put a kind of drain stopper on the dig—you
know—like the rubber ones for a tub. You
imagine now that if you take it off too soon,

everything inside will flow out—guts and
lungs and brains and blood and bones.
It's the Fentanyl again, and at first
the notion seems a nightmare, then
changes over to a fantasy, a wish—
to hear the echoes of the climax fade away.

# CORONA

How dare it interfere with your deathless,
deathy Poesy! You have done your best
for two months now to disregard this mastodon
outside the room, breathing its foul
vapors upon your fugitive and cloistered
aerie of in-place sheltering, to say nothing
of the entire world. But here it is,
in an effort to elbow out (if mastodons
have elbows) for one poem, at least,
the main attraction in this sickness circus—you.
So deal with it, make it part of the show,
because it is. Because it has to be,
however hideous it is, and it is very.

Sickness is the link, Mr. Duh. The one
tailored for the individual, the other
for the world. The latter survivable—98–99%—
the former sloppy-looking little nightmare
somewhat less so—5%? 3%? And those no doubt
misdiagnoses in the first place.

You are microscopic but also microcosmic—
some comfort, of however cold a kind.
At this time in particular, illness is a tie
that binds, and so. You pray your agnostic
prayers not only for yourself but for
the entire shivering, sweating world—

a compulsory-attendance carnival
of happenstance with no ringmaster or
flyers—just a midway.

## WORM MOON

You're back upon the chemo throne:
a reclinable, foot-restable, hummus-colored,
would-be treatment E-Z chair, in this
case wouldn't-be, couldn't-be—because
of why you're here: more than an hour's
worth of chemotherapy, mainly
at the hands of gemcitabine, a crystal-clear
infusion of a chemical to slow
the growth of what's eating and will
end up killing you before the next
Worm Moon.

(So named because that's when
the worms that had been gorging on
what was left of you have risen to
the thaw and are worming all around,
the worm gavotte, with not a thought
in the heads that they, the luckies, lack).

So: What to do with your own head, as you're
infused? You can't read anything with
continuity, because your own
is being eaten up so fast. But you
have your phone and can look things up,
which, along with this, is what you have
been doing with these racing days.

Gemcitabine, eh? Let's see (*trans.*:
Wikipedia): Whoa plus Eureka!
Take a look at this, from the long
entry in our shortcutter's first resort:

As of 2017, gemcitabine was marketed under many brand names worldwide: Abine, Accogem, Acytabin, Antoril, axigem, Bendacitabin, Biogem, Boligem, Celzar, Citegin, Cytigem, Cytogem, Daplax, DBL, Demozar, Dercin, Emcitab, Enekamub, Eriogem, Fotinex, Gebina, Gemalata, Gembin, Gembine, Gembio, Gemcel, Gemcetin, Gemcibine, Gemcikal, Gemcipen, Gemcired, Gemcirena, Gemcit, Gemcitabin, Gemcitabina, Gemcitabine, Gemcitabinum, Gemcitan, Gemedac, Gemflor, Gemful, Gemita, Gemko, Gemliquid, Gemmis, Gemnil, Gempower, Gemsol, Gemstad, Gemstada, Gemtabine, Gemtavis, Gemtaz, Gemtero, Gemtra, Gemtro, Gemvic, Gemxit, Gemzar, Gentabim, Genuten, Genvir, Geroam, Gestredos, Getanosan, Getmisi, Gezt, Gitrabin, Gramagen, Haxanit, Jemta, Kalbezar, Medigem, Meditabine, Nabigem, Nallian, Oncogem, Oncoril, Pamigeno, Ribozar, Santabin, Sitagem, Symtabin, Yu Jie, Ze Fei, and Zefei

The hideous "Enekamub," like the evil names
in Gilgamesh. "Gemalata"—a flavor of gelato.
"Gestredos," a safe drug for the pregnant.
"Meditabine," for the contemplative,
"Gemliquid," for the literal-minded,
"Nallian," for patients from Armenia,
"Santabin," administered at Christmas,
and "Haxanit," a bug spray gone astray.

You Search and Search, but nowhere can
you find an etymology for the
generic "gemcitabine." There must be
a chemical explanation, you are sure.
You imagine some lab guy
shouting out "Eureka!—I have
the name at last: 'gemcitabine'!"

Don't you have enough to worry on?
And anyway, a rose by any other name
(except, perhaps, Daplax), et cetera.
Our languages—the way our brains must work—
require us to believe that what we say
is a welded part of what it designates.
It's not. This kind of thing,
if it's any good, is the closest we can come
to making words sound instrumental,
to make them be what they name.

## WHAT'S SO FUNNY?

In the kitchen, decades ago, you drop
an egg. You lean over, with a quiet "Fuck!,"
to clean it up, and from
behind comes "hyuh-hyuh-hyuh-hyuh-hyuh"
from his highchair, Will's first laugh—
at five months and your expense,
but you laugh, too, and wonder how he—
how we—know how to start to laugh.

In fourth grade, the teacher asks if
someone knows the names of Columbus's
three ships. Up goes Roberta's hand.
"The Atchison, Topeka, and the Santa Fe."
We laugh, those of us who understand
not only what went wrong but on
some instinctive level how it's right:
the threeness, the scansion, the overlapping
Santas, and the land-and-sea conveyances.

In college, in a soccer game, a substitute
for the other side fields a throw-in and begins
to dribble in the wrong direction. He
corrects it right away, but both sides laugh
a little, and the game goes on.

At work, in publishing, you keep a list
of orthographic errors of high quality:

esprit décor, kneed in the walnuts, Al
Italia called, from the gecko, gets my
gander up, ultraviolent radiation.
You laugh each time you look at them.

You have always wondered what's
so funny about anything you think
is funny. As the gemcitabine drips its last
few drops, to knock you down, Nurse Luddy
accidentally drops her cellphone
into the trash. You both laugh, and
then, after what is fast and so unfairly
approaching an entire lifetime, you get it.
All previous ideas about humor fly
into that same trash. You have the answer:

We are cast ashore here on the beach
of life without the faintest idea why.
Because there is no reason and no plan
that we can ever know. Your mother
had a headache on that climactic
night? No you. Mine? No me. Federer's?
No he. Golda Meier's? Presley's? His dad's?

We are accidents. We know that,
even if we tell ourselves we don't.
So what we laugh at, even when it's "planned,"
is always accidental, and at its heart about
our predicament.

Any pratfall is our pratfall.
Any knock-knock joke is about our fears.
Gorilla walks into a bar? What
could be more random?
The universe has no truck with fairness.
There's nothing unfair about my
situation. Nothing unfair about yours.
Bad, maybe. Horrendous, even,
arbitrary, unwarranted. But
if we are not in too much pain or peril,
the only thing to do is laugh.
(You'll see how that holds up when you are dying.)

Nurse Luddy drops her phone *again*.
Guess what we both do.

# LUCK

At home that night you cannot sleep—a
paradox of the extreme fatigue brought on
by treatment. (Not unusual: in all the warnings.)
Your wife beside you turns over, begins her
quiet—ladylike but audible—respiring.
You go back to happenstance, as
a dreary consolation for your suffering,
and your fate. But it turns around on you,
as if it knows it has another job to do.

What have we here! Why, it's the Village
in the forties—stoopball, Creamsicles,
baseball cards, a lefty private school—
the aptronymic Little Red School House.
Music taught by Charity Bailey (*q.*G).
Jennifer Warren, an actress later, shows
you how to kiss. Lead Belly at the Village
Gate, your older brother, Mike, boyhandling
you but unable to match your insults.

And here!—Nyack High School, different
altogether. It turns out that here you are
an athlete of sorts, and, even more surprising,
one of the boys. You are Schnoz (your nose
has grown to betray the half-Jew in you), your
friends are Roach, Sleepy, Numb Thumb, Board,

your girlfriend Pam, whose father drives the bus
that takes your parents to the city and their work.
Much mischief here—stealing 45s,
paying Crazy John to buy beer for
you, the underaged, learning with
delight that Doc Lloyd, the trainer,
and his friend, Mr. Griz, a coach
(married to a hideous gay-camouflage
wife) who purposely hit you in the balls
during batting practice, have left town
overnight, when the janitor, after school,
discovered Doc blowing Badboy Kelly
in the locker room.

At this rate you will never finish this,
which cannot take the hour or so
that the Luck Reminders are taking
now. So: College: Mr. Hynes:
fighter pilot, Yeats admirer ("Why
Does Yeats say "*slow* thighs" in 'The Second
Coming'?") Grad School: Professor
Wasserman hammering home his
"subject-object" theory of the Romantics.
High-school teaching: yearbook dedicated to
guess who. After that: magazines and
publishing and writing. The best thing there?
Easy: Alice Munro. And, writ large,
**your marriage and your kids.** The State Department
trips to Georgia, the country, and

Nepal. Nepal! Where you can buy a "driver's
license" on the street from a disheveled vendor.

You worked for much of this, but even
the ability to do the work
is luck. Total it up, weigh it on
the scales whose other disc holds
a fatal illness, and the winner is
the good. A good innings, as the
British say—it's better for its
implication of an adversary.

So now, despite the little nausea
that troubles your interiors, they decide
to let you sleep. But not without
a few bad dreams—one that has you driving
on a narrow one-way street: The
wheel has its own ideas, taking
you from side to side, millimeters
from some savage scraping and being
scraped by this parked car or that.
But even in your sleep you know
that this is what you, what we,
must go through to obey the rules
of luck's unbalanced equilibrium.

The memory of the good-luck cavalcade
stays with you in the morning, for
a little while.

PART V

# TERMINALIA

## LAST WILL AND TESTAMENT

Are you hoping for a laugh up there,
my friend the Poet? "Only for myself,"
you reply. "Another toasting in
the microwave tomorrow. Getting tired
of this. The end is close enough to make
it closer. What's the point of going on?"
To keep you here as long as possible.
You would be missed, you know.
"Will be" is what you say. "Unfortunately,
there's not a thing conditional about it.
And I won't be. Missed, that is—
Not by many or for long.

"I've made internal peace with four
who've wronged me grievously.
I've made external peace with all the rest
and they with me, I hope. A grudge gains
weight with age. Get rid of it. Die lighter.
We are each of us a flotilla
of virtue, shame, honor, pride,
hatefulness—not the single bark we
think we are. And anyway, these four did no
more or less than what they had to do.
We believe we make our choices. but no—
they make us."

## COMPUTERIZED PTOMOGRAPHY

In you go, on the narrow, sliding bed. Slab? What?
(You look it up later: "Translating couch"?
Really?) "Hold your breath," says some ghost
in the machine, in a subdued dictator's tone.
The little face on the narrow little screen above
the tube into which you're being translated
shuts its little mouth, which had been . . . open.
"Aye aye," you think, and shut your
much bigger one—always a challenge.

Inside the cylinder, some kind of
mechanism in a window above your
body begins to whir and turn. Ten seconds,
maybe? You're retro-translated, and "Breathe,"
says the little sergeant ghost, its
icon's mouth open once again.

You feel as limited and boring here as the
little ghost must feel. Your "clever" titles
for this poem and the one before:
products of a kind of desperation.
You can't go out—the virus is still hard
at work, apparently immune to boredom.
"Infect, infect, infect, infect"—
a limited repertoire, the same
as most mass murderers.

You can't see Will and Lizi, for whom
at this point you and Katherine have done
close to all you can. Or for K, herself,
who you're sure at least has thought about
contingencies. Entertainment—whose roots
mean "hold together"—has lost, for you, its power
of adhesive. Even doing this has—like
you yourself, as you look into the
mirror that covers up your
prescription-ridden cabinet—
begun to pale.

And here's the pain again—referred
up from that distended pancreas of yours
into your clavicle—the left one, this time, not
the right. Along with dizziness you get
your pedant's tiny kick from remembering
the adjective for "clavicle"—"clavicular."
But man oh man are you ever pale!
And what's with this cold sweat, nausea, and diz

## TODD BLANKSTEIN

He lives alone across the street from me
in Erie County, very near the lake—
the shallowest of the five but with
the fiercest winds.
His name is on the mailbox—
at which, as with
my own, the mailman
never even has to break his stride.

From time to time Todd knocks softly
on my door and asks to "borrow"
half a cup of vinegar, or a little salt.
And, once, "Do you have an onion
you can spare?" Another time, some mustard,
another, Baker's Chocolate,
another (with a laugh), a little Drano.
And, summer before last, a pair of clippers—
not yet returned.

Why he comes to me and not the other
neighbors is a puzzle. Is there something
special here? In any case, I don't mind—
In fact, I like him, in a way.
He parks his sheet-white truck behind his house,
is busy with it night and day, day and night,
in and out, out and in. Its freight remains
a mystery to me and all the neighbors

on the block. Or so I guess—I
don't know them well. Well, actually, at all.

What really gets me is his garden. I've
never seen him work it, but in the
spring it erupts so gorgeously with
tulips, iris, pansies, purple stock, and
daffodils—and poppies, many, many poppies,
all oddly oversize.

What is even stranger is
the way he disregards his own
soil's artistry. And, stranger yet,
every now and then, these recent days,
he takes my clippers out there (he used to use
his hand—the left), and after careful
scrutiny he clips this flower or that,
throws it on the ground, and walks away.

In the winter, when his garden's bleak and brown
and full of scrub, he sits out there, underdressed,
in a red and worn-out patio chair,
and drinks a glass or two—of what,
I'd really like to know.
Now it's April. I, for one,
am looking forward to a quiet spring
atop a peaceful winter of this work
But right now, there's the little knock.
It's Todd—who else?—with my clippers

in his hand. (The right one now.)
"This is not my custom, but you've been
very kind to me" is what he says.
"Therefore we should talk, I think."

## ACKNOWLEDGMENTS

First and fivemost, thank you to Katha Pollitt, an utterly brilliant poet and a cherished friend. Wise, funny, astonishingly self-aware, politically super-astute, and with a candor that sometimes seems to take even herself by surprise, she was an early reader of this work and was so encouraging as to keep me at it during a time of travail. She gets a paragraph all to herself, and it's not enough.

Thank you to my wife, Katherine Bouton, who has supported me in this endeavor, while leading the New York City Chapter of the Hearing Loss Association of America for years with firmness, fairness, and creativity. She has stood by me through thick and a great deal of thin, and has borne my temper and despair with patience and love. Thank you to my children, Will and Lizi, the headlights of my life. They have made me proud almost to the point of explosion.

Thank you to all my friends—Sam Douglas, David Nasaw, Deborah Garrison, Leo Braudy, James Gleick, and many others, especially Charles McGrath, also an early reader. He predicted that this book would sell 200,000 copies. (The cash register is over there, near the entrance but a little hard to find. Here—I'll show you.)

Thank you to everyone at *n+1*, especially Marco Roth, Mark Krotov, and Rachel Ossip, who came up with the arresting design and layout for this book. Thank you to Gillian MacKenzie, who has represented (and in some cases edited) this work with not only professionalism but warmth and understanding. Thank you to Dr. Anna Varghese, at Memorial Sloan Kettering, for her smart and supportive care. And thank you to you, catholic enough to even just pick up a book of poetry about pancreatic cancer, for Christ's sake.

## ABOUT THE POET

Daniel Menaker was the author of seven books, two of them among the *New York Times'* Best Books of the Year, another an Editors' choice. He twice won the O. Henry Award for short stories, and his fiction, essays, and reporting appeared in the *New Yorker*, the *New York Times*, *Harper's*, *The Atlantic*, *n+1*, *Vogue*, *Esquire*, and many other publications, including *Country Music Magazine* and the *New Marlborough Five Village News*. He also served as an editor at the *New Yorker* for two decades and as executive editor-in-chief of Random House, working with Alice Munro, William Trevor, George Saunders, Matthew Klam, Renata Adler, John McPhee, Pauline Kael, Janet Malcolm, Elizabeth Strout, Jennifer Egan, David Foster Wallace, Michael Chabon, Billy Collins, Deborah Garrison, Virginia Hamilton Adair, Reza Aslan, Max Frisch, Stanislaw Lem, Shirley Hazzard, Salman Rushdie, Sister Helen Prejean, Siddhartha Mukherjee, Mavis Gallant, Gary Shteyngart, Raymond Carver, and Elmore Leonard. He was a member of the Board of the Poetry Foundation for several years and also tutored reading and writing in New York City public schools.

He is survived by his wife Katherine Bouton, a former editor at the *New York Times* and the author of three books on hearing loss, and their two children, Will Menaker—a founder and co-host of the podcast *Chapo Trap House*—and Elizabeth Menaker, a psychotherapist. He graduated from Swarthmore College with High Honors, earned a master's degree in English Literature from Johns Hopkins University, and taught English for five years before going to work as a fact checker at the *New Yorker*.

He wrote poetry his whole life, but kept it to himself for a long time, after being told by William Maxwell, his otherwise kindly teacher at the *New Yorker*, "Stick to prose."